Outspoken

J. L. Hansen

iUniverse, Inc.
Bloomington

Outspoken

iUniverse books may be ordered through booksellers or by contacting:

iUniverse
1663 Liberty Drive
Bloomington, IN 47403
www.iuniverse.com
1-800-Authors (1-800-288-4677)

ISBN: 978-1-4620-3362-1 (sc)
ISBN: 978-1-4620-3363-8 (e)

Printed in the United States of America

iUniverse rev. date: 07/18/2011

Outspoken

a.   candid or bold in speech

b.   said or expressed with boldness

Thank you!

Thank you all that supported me from the very beginning of Vindicated and those who have joined me on this journey. Thank You to Veronika Erickson for keeping your imagination on edge through this project. Thank you to my guest artists, each one of you inspire me to think bigger. Big thank you to Clint Bailey, Zia Ajeti, Emma Brown, Rose Mary Húeramo and Jayme Watkins for listening to me complain through this experience. Thank you to my family for their love & unconditional support! A special thank you to my guardian angel, Ella you are still in my heart & will be forever.

All photos were taken by
Veronika Erickson & **J. L. Hansen**.

This is for Lacey Elizabeth.
Never change, you're beautiful the way you are.

I don't know how to be quiet
But most importantly
I don't want to be…
I'd rather be **OUTSPOKEN**

Now please travel with me through a journey of my uncapped thoughts…

Please keep arms inside at all times…

Thank you & Enjoy!

Outspoken

This Time 1

New Chapter. 3

Unchained. 4

Puppets Pulled Into Pulpits 5

The Feeling 6

Ingredients of Me 7

My Past Demons. 8

Never Follow. 9

Inspire Me Raw. 11

Pretty Girl. 12

The Naked Truth. 14

Tell Me 15

Laugh 16

Smile. 18

Repeat. 20

Beautiful Mess. 22

Beauty. 24

The death of the shattered 25

Sometimes. 26

Tetris. 27

Cuz 28

Give Me Something Real. 30

My Style, My Heart, My Words 32

He Guides. 34

News Flash 36

HATE. 38

I believe. 41

Are We There Yet? 42

Body & Mind & Heart & Soul. 43

Love in the Now 45

Dreams 46

Color me a Picture 47

Lie to Me 48

One Fire 49

Build Up. 51

Me 52

Outspoken 53

Everything. 54

LOVE. 55

Enter at Your Own Risk 56

Revolution with blackened fingernails. 58

Free Me. 59

That Girl. 60

Hey Boy!. 61

Girl with the Bulldog 63

What We Make It 65

The exhausted admiration of self worth. . . . 66

This Time

I'm following my heart
I'm making my own rules
I'm making my own decisions
I'm not taking no for an answer
I'm not doing it for you
I'm not giving up
I'm giving it my all
Last time I gave you the power
This time I'm taking back what is mine

New Chapter

Depression: behind me

Suicide: weak idea

Bipolar: wrongly accused

Hate: from time to time

Anger: an emotion we all feel

The past is what makes us who we are

Lets learn from it and keep moving forward

Unchained

Bored of following the rules
Tired of striving for unreachable perfection
Sick of being told "NO!"
Numb from only feeling hate
Uninterested in failing again and again
In this moment I am unchained
I am unbound
I am liberated
I am limitless
I am open-minded
I am uncontrolled
I am free

Puppets Pulled Into Pulpits
Zachary A. Gunning

Human beings as a whole are essentially puppets pulled into pulpits. For the world to yank it's hefty strain of strings forecasting humanity's unforgiving glare. Denial of one's failures becomes an unfortunate necessity, and acceptance brings a frown upon the face of humanity. Look beneath the layers of social mediocrity, and you shall convene the truth. In the end, our existence only brings a unique warped sense of the blueprint to become just another puppet. Manipulated & cast aside the moment you have no longer any use for me. I yearn for your acceptance, knowing that's a byproduct I'll never gain. I have no father, you are my preacher.

The Feeling
Lacey Elizabeth Munch

The feeling when
It all breaks down
When you know its
Going to end
When everything tumbles
To the ground.
The feeling tells all
This is the part
Where you say its
Over and I say
It's your loss
Not mine
Everyone says you
Don't deserve me
I'm starting to think
They may be right
The feeling tells all...

Ingredients of Me

The rumor is that little girls are made of sugar spice and everything nice.
But this one is made of something else.
Dash of shock
Tablespoon of random
Cupful of creativity
Handful of volume
Teaspoon of laughter
Pound of energy
Pinch of Self-expression
Shake don't stir
Bake for half hour on low

My Past Demons

Somewhere I have found the strength & the courage to let go
Close the door on all my past demons
Look forward not backwards
Visit memories but not live in them

Never Follow

Stop
Now
Go
Speed
Now
Slow
Lead
Never
Follow
Just
Let
Go

Inspire Me Raw

Color me red
Inspire me raw
Giggle me happy
Tickle me pink
Joke me tenderly
Hurt me never
Sing me loudly
Tell me slowly
Kiss me sweetly
Love me endlessly
Surrender me never
Hold me forever
Nothing else will do
For I only want to be with you

Pretty Girl
Lauren Alicia

Pretty girl you deserve more than this
Pretty girl you shouldn't let him treat you like that
I know you think that you're in love
But love is patient and love is kind

Pretty girl he's trying to mess with your head
Pretty girl he'll hurt you again
I know he's saying that he loves you and how sorry he is
But please pretty girl don't you believe him

Cause you are beautiful
And you have a heart of gold
You don't need some boy to tell you
Who you are
Pretty girl

Pretty girl you're worth more than this
Pretty girl don't sell yourself for tips
I know you think that this is all that you are good for
But please pretty girl don't you believe that

Cause you are beautiful
And you have a heart of gold
You don't need no one to tell you
Who you are
Pretty Girl

Promise me next time you look in the mirror
You'll drown out all the voices telling you that you aren't
Smart enough brave enough strong enough
Cool enough Sexy enough Pretty enough
When you are

Pretty girl I know it feels like your world is caving in
And letting go is easier than facing it
But be strong keep holding on
And you'll see how pretty you are

Cause you are beautiful
And you have a heart of gold
You don't need no one to tell you
Who you are
Pretty Girl

The Naked Truth

Ritchie Martinez

You're not gonna like it but I swear it's true...
I'm out of your zeitgeist and in the light
I'm inside the moment and out of my mind
I desecrate your holy walls with my true colors
I penetrate your world with my reality
I smash your flashing boxes that tell me who to be
I look into your eyes and what I see is me
I only wear genetic makeup
I have nothing to hide
I stand before you naked
For you to judge and criticize
So swallow the pill
Red or blue
Can you handle the truth?
It's up to you.

Tell Me

What is the sound of your happiness?
What is the motive of your passion?
What is the taste of your treat?
What is the face of your inspiration?
What is the joy in your heart?
What is the color of your soul?
Now tell me…
What is the purpose of your life?

Laugh

Smile out loud
Laugh often
Giggle with a snort
Chuckle for no reason
Grin at a favorite memory
Smirk without a sound
Beam inside and out
Make the most out of every moment

Smile

Smile on cue for the camera
Smile big for the world
Smile loudly for your friends
Smile nervously for the unknown
Smile genuinely for yourself

Repeat

Sleep
Eat
Dance
Repeat

Live
Laugh
Love
Repeat

Inhale
Exhale
Smile
Repeat

Repeat until you're satisfied
Repeat until you feel alive

Beautiful Mess

Unorganized
Disorder
Skewed
Chaos
Clutter
Untidiness
Misaligned
Everything that's not perfect
Everything you hate
Everything you run from
Everything you won't admit
Everything you are scared of
Everything I am

Beauty

What is beauty?
Is it only skin deep?
Does it change?
Does it grow?
Does it wan?
Does it wax?
Is it a size 2?
Does it have a size?
Does it have a color?
Does it have a height?
Beauty is unchanged confidence
Beauty is an assurance of who you are when others try to
break you down
Beauty is changing for no one
Beauty has no size, no color, no height
Beauty is what we make it

The death of the shattered
Doug Reaves

He writes of the scenes that play throughout his imagination. His words are a symphony of perfect pitch and they paint portraits of renaissance beauty. He describes a world of ignorant innocence only challenged by the desires of a woman of whom he has never known. She has skin as smooth as hand spun silk and with eyes the color of spiring skies she stares into the souls of the unloved. She protects him. She is his angel of glass, comprised of delicate crystal and ever-lasting understanding. Through his words, she is real. He writes of her and she makes him a poet amongst dead men. Only a pen of black ink and paper with rounded edges keep him from joining the fallen. He sits in a space of solid brick bounded by rusted steel with only himself to keep clean.

Sometimes

Sometimes I lie
Sometimes I speak before I think
Sometime I say naughty words
Sometimes I say mean things
Sometimes I shout!
Sometimes I speak harshly
Sometimes I say the wrong thing
But no matter what I say
I always say something

Tetris

Fitting the blocks together perfectly to get ahead
Using the gifts we have received without question of why
we got them
Making chaos look easy and almost beautiful
Moving swiftly without error
Is this Tetris or life

Cuz

Pink cuz I'm a girl
Attitude cuz I want to
Spunk cuz it's more fun
Love cuz I choose
Peace cuz I believe
Passion cuz I feel it
Change cuz I want it
Cuz I can!

Give Me Something Real

The diamonds are shiny but they don't interest me
The dollars are crisp but they are only paper
The cars are fast but I'm a bad driver
Give me something real
Not superficial
Give me words
Give me passion
Give me Love
Give me something real
Not superficial

My Style, My Heart, My Words

My style's my own with a dash of punk for show
My heart is pure with real emotions
My thoughts are complex with simple fears
My words are short with genuine panic
My expression is straightforward with complication
I'd rather be anything than fake
I'd rather be anything than counterfeit
I'd rather be anything than plastic
I'd rather be anything than molded

He Guides

You run one way
Then abruptly change course
You follow
Then
You lead
Redirect
You look back but never go back
You stay on track
You have faith

News Flash

News flash one of the largest sex symbols EVER...Marilyn
Monroe:
5'5"
118 lbs
dress size 12
pant size 8
bra size 36D
this was BEFORE plastic surgery

my sizes:
5'7"
148 lbs
pant size 11
dress size 9
bra size 36 C

I'm sorry but I refuse to have gay men and anorexic women
tell me I'm not attractive because I'm not a size 2!!
I vow here and now to be happy and confident in my own
skin!
I am choosing to not let the media make me feel unpretty.

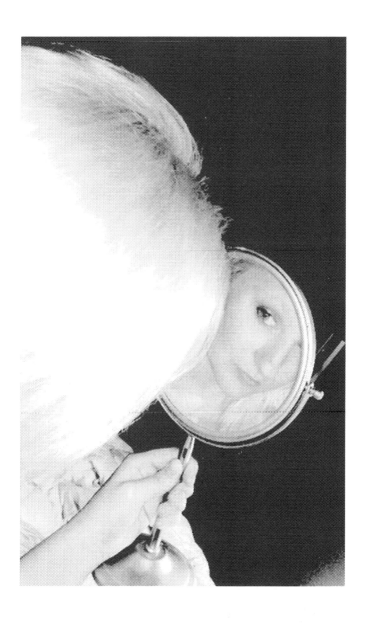

HATE

I hate when I run into a wall that has been in the same spot for years

I hate when I trip on air

I hate that you're too pretty for me

I hate that I fall in love at least twice a day but never fall out of love

I hate when people complain about the rain

I hate when people laugh when I'm serious

I hate that people don't understand my sense of humor

I hate that my laugh can make a dog's eardrum burst

I hate when people don't take me seriously because of my age

I hate when I over analyze your last text

I hate that she looks up to me when I'm not a good role model

I hate that I chip my nails when I play my guitar

I hate that my gaydar is off and I can't reset it

I hate that no one understands my musical references

I hate it when you try to censor me

I hate that I'm a city girl living in the country

I hate when the kid next to me in class thinks I'm flirting with him when I ask if we had homework

I hate when people ask me if I'm drunk when I'm sober

I hate when people ask me to be quiet

I hate that I feel like I'm late when I'm five minutes early
I may have many imperfections
But I love my life!
I would not want it any other way!

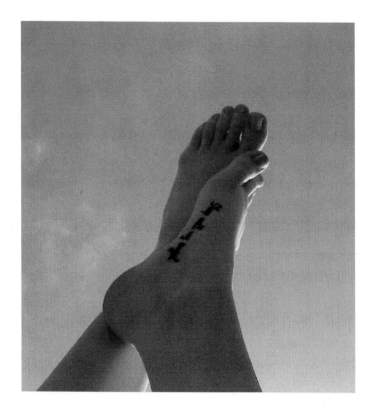

I believe...

One little voice can make a big difference
One chance can change the whole world
One step can lead to many
One smile can save a life
What do you believe?

Are We There Yet?

Inside
Outside
Sideways
Left ways
Right ways
This way
That way
Your way
My way
We'll find our way!

Body & Mind & Heart & Soul

Self-assured
And
Beautiful

Confident
And
Classy

Bold
And
Brilliant

Strong
And
Resilient

Body & Mind & Heart & Soul

Love in the Now

Giggling

Smiling

Glowing

Shining

Sparkling

Cheerful

Joyful

Blissful

Stay this way forever

Love looks good on you

Dreams

I use to think dreams were only for the weak
The helpless
The powerless
The broken
Thanks to you
Now I realize dreams are for the hopeful
Quitting is for the weak

Color me a Picture

Color me a picture of a place
Where love never dies
Laughter is always loud
Hope never fades
Glory never alters
Faith never expires
Beauty is always raw
Trust is always true
Friendship never parishes
Color me a picture

Lie to Me

Sing me perfection
Draw me excellence
Tell me faultlessness
Write me rightness
Build me flawlessness
Color me exactness
Lie to me if you have to

One Fire

One match
One flame
Turns into...
One fire
Destroying everything
Leaving no survivors
Capturing all prisoners
Consuming life
Leaving poison
But hope still remains
Tomorrow is anew

Build Up

Why tear each other down
When we can build each other up?
Why hurt each other
When we can heal each other?
Why hate each other
When we can love each other?

Me

I'm not who I want to be
I'm not who I used to be
I'm not where I want to be
I'm not where I used to be
I will become who I need to be
I will become who I'm suppose to be
I will forgive the old me
I will love the new me

Outspoken

I could try and be tame
But that's no fun!
I could attempt to be normal
But what is normal?
I could strive for perfection
But who is perfect?
I could struggle to make you happy
But I honestly don't care if you are!
I could strain to be quiet
But I'd rather be OUTSPOKEN!

Everything
Lacey Elizabeth Munch

I saw you
I met you
I liked you
I dated you
I loved you
I lost you
I hated you
I missed you
I contacted you
I like you again
I love you again
I now realize you're everything I need

LOVE

Living the life I love
Overlooking flaws to find love
Volunteering my heart for love
Enduring the ups and down while fighting for love

Enter at Your Own Risk

I'll be your poison for the night
I'll be the heroin you inject into your bloodstream
I'll be the stake that's driven into your heart
I'll be the bait that awaits in the cage
I'll be the girl that robs your love
I'll be the dream that you can never possess
You'll be the brainless one who tries to stay
You'll be the slow learner who cannot understand
You'll be a forgotten memory
You'll be an easy target for a bitch like me
You'll be a pawn in my little girly game
You'll be a prisoner locked in my lonely chambers
I'm laying it out clearly for you…
I'm just being honest…
You cannot say I never warned you!

Revolution with blackened fingernails
Doug Reaves

In a room built for fine theater stands a stage under a steel truss covered in multi colored par cans.

Beams of red, blue and green cascade down on a mad man with a microphone who shouts words of revolution to a mob of abused youth.

Stage left are six strings that produce orchestrated sonic anarchy in rhythm with a pulsating hypnotic kick drum that pounds like a right hook of a prize fighter through the rib cages of the members of the mob.

Outside, the city sleeps while inside the abused dance in unison as if they were members of a militia marching to a knife fight.

The walls of the room drip the sweat of rage and the cigarette smoke is thick like fog.

Free Me

It's the rumble
It's the tumble
It's the rustle
It's the bustle
It's the rain
It's the pain
It's my dear
It's my fear
It's my sin
It's my skin
It's my love
It's the dove
It's the craze
It's a phase
It's a breeze
It's an ease
It's your beauty
It's my duty
It's my mess
It's my stress
It's your grace
It's this place
That I need
That I want
That keeps me going
That keeps me alive
That sets me free!

That Girl

I'm the kind of girl that will make you think twice
I'm the kind of girl that will make you cry
I'm the kind of girl that will make you man up
I'm the kind of girl that will change how you view life
I'm the kind of girl that will make you wish you never met me
I'm the kind of girl that will make you a better person
I'm the kind of girl that you can fall in love with & will fall in love with you
I'm the kind of girl that will want to dance in the rain with you
I'm the kind of girl you will not want to leave
I'm just that kind of girl

Hey Boy!

Hey Boy this is me
I'm not the kind of girl that spends her life in a shopping mall
I need adventure
I was kicked out of the girl's club when I traded in my
Barbie's for Hot Wheels
I wasn't accepted by the boy's club because I didn't have
a Y chromosome
I am a simple girl in this crazy world
I don't need diamonds and pearls I just need attention
I am ADHD so I'm hard to keep up with
I've been told I'm a handful
Hey Boy
Can you handle me?

Girl with the Bulldog

I'm not a Diva
I'm not perfect
I'm not a dream
I'm not a princess
I'm not an angel
I never claimed to be
I'm just a girl with a bulldog

What We Make It

It's an emotion
It's a feeling
It's a thought
It's an illness
It's an expression
It's a right
It's a song
It's a wish
It's an image
It's a concern
It's a cancer
It's a fear
It's a love
It's a want
It's a cause
It's an effect
It's a reaction
It's what we make it

The exhausted admiration of self worth
Doug Reaves

The northern suburbs of the city swam in the abyss of dead dreams and lost romance. When all hope is gone, people need a savior. someone to rise from the crushed earth with a sword of strength and ideas of social and economic revolution. This messiah will have the mind of a mad man and the courage of a warrior. He will bleed the blood of gods and bathe in the sweat of the poor. He will take from the wealthy and give to the dark souls that make up the burnt wastelands that now cover the fallen cities. Born of human flesh, he lives only in literature as a chosen hero for all to believe in. Civilization slowly burns like rich tobacco from a fine cigarette while our hero counts the moments until the canvas is wiped clean. He will paint a picture of purity. The grass will grow again and the sun will rise. This day will come. Our savior will arrive.

On the corner of a broken street on the east side of town sat a dive bar where the local blue collar gentlemen would quench their depression with cheap domestic brew. The bartender had age upon her face beyond the years of her time. She wore the wounds of social decline on her forehead and her eyes were the color of ash smeared upon crystal. She was thin but her clothes were reminders of the days before the hunger. She served her patrons with sinister glares of sarcasm and a dry humorless wit. There were no more stories anymore. She chose to retire the sounds of the jukebox in exchange for silence. She enjoyed the bitter commentary of the local work force. The bar top was old and in need of refinishing. It was scared with the imprints of elbows and covered with the rings of pint glasses. The dense smoke of the working mans cowboy killers consumed the room and generations of mans regrets were soaked deep within the walls. The mood was always somber. Every day was much the same. Whether it was the rumblings of revolt against the high fuel prices, the inconsistent employment rate, or the lack of natural resources, the shallow remains of the working man never were at a loss for words. This local dive was where all the reminders of the grim reality were housed and cared for a beaten bartender.

It was a weekday. The calendar read Tuesday, the 12th day of March. The snow outside was beginning to melt thanks to the bright sun in the early afternoon sky. The bar was open and a few of the regular patrons were already on their stools with a brew in hand. The bartender was in a lively mood this day. She had woken up that morning to the news of a new death. This death killed with out regard for the dignity of man. It struck without warning and before you could even scream your sickness, it bled your tongue and ate away at your muscles. It was all over the mass media circus of cable, satellite television, internet web browsers and smart phone news applications. The educated had concluded that this was a manmade death for which man could not fight and only through years of evolution could we build a defense. The bartender had a love affair with the overcast that had been building over existence and epidemics like this made her smile more than any man ever could.

As the day faded, the evening gloom was in its infant stage when the bar door swung open with the speed of elderly foot steps. The bartender took notice to the shadow that stood in the doorway. This man was not one of her men. He was tall, or least he stood tall. He had broad shoulders and walked toward the bar with purpose. As the faint light from the dim table lamps illuminated his features, his supreme confidence was revealed through his eyes that seemed to be constructed by the pages of history books. He was a healthy thin and appeared strong. His hair was brown with the tint of moist sand. It was short, just enough length slicked back as if he had just come from a big business board meeting. He was clean shaven and wore the clothing of a simple man. He was not a working man for his hands were smooth and free of the burdens that plagued the patrons of the bar. The bartender was consumed by the presence of the stranger as he took a seat on a broken stool at the bar. She was curious as to what could bring such a man to her bar of shattered progress. This was the place where the fallen turned forgotten. This was no place for a man with fair skin and a clean conscious.

"Could I trouble you for a water?" said the stranger.

He made direct eye contact with the bartender when he spoke. This was a man of pride. No man who frequents this bar would ever look the bartender in the eye. They are broken men without the strength to show respect.

"Sure thing stranger. Are you sure you just want water? My boys usually require something a little stronger in order to survive the nights."

The stranger didn't even crack so much as a smirk. He just kept his eyes on the bartender and responded without hesitation.

"Water quenches the body, the brew distorts the mind. I'm just thirsty."

The bartender was not used to this sort of conversation. Any words beyond that of a drink order were never spoken here.

"So stranger, I've never seen you here before and I know every one of my drunks. What brings ya in to town?"

This was more than just small talk. Something about her visitor intrigued the bartender. He spoke with education and unlike the men around him his voice did not quiver or shake. She was never one to ask questions of her regulars. She honestly didn't care for their answers so she figured just serve the drinks and take the money. This stranger was different. His very stature demanded attention and explanation. This was no place for this stranger.

"I'm just passing through on business and figured I'd get a look and feel for the place. I travel a lot and one thing I've learned through all my travels is that if you really want to get to know some place in a hurry, go to where the drinks are cheap and the company is honest."

"Well, I do take some pride in being honest mister, so I gotta tell ya that there aint nothing you can learn from this dive. I listen to these boys gripe and complain all day every day bout the shit they gotta do, the shit they wanna do, and the shit they can't do. Trust me when I tell ya, I aint learned shit from this place", replied the bartender in a sharp, sarcastic tone.

"Well miss, I believe that there is more to your surroundings than what is on the surface. The men that come in here and complain as you say, are actually telling you a story. Each complaint is a chapter in the epic tale of this town. Perhaps they come here because they are looking for someone to proofread their chapter and help them mold it to the way they read it in their own mind."

The stranger spoke with a distinct arrogance. He kept his back straight and his posture was perfect with every word.

"I don't wanna be rude here mister, but be careful about using that word "believe" in this place. There aint much belief left 'round here let alone something to even believe in. You watch the news or read the paper at all mister? You hear 'bout the new mystery disease that be killing folks? They say that it was created by man. With shit like that goin' on, belief in anything 'round here is gonna be hard to find."

"I've heard of this new death. When the unexplained threatens the delicate order of progress, belief and hope are the only things one can turn to for guidance", answered the stranger, again without hesitation.

The education from which the stranger spoke didn't sit well with the bartender. This man was not like the men who come in her bar and throw back domestic brew and snack on the stale pretzels she leaves on the tables. This stranger didn't appear to have the hunger.

The stranger took a sip from his glass of water and again looked the bartender in the eye.

"May I ask you a question?" asked the stranger of the bartender.

"A question? Well aint this a surprise. No one ever asks me much of nothin'. Go ahead mister, ask away."

"What have you learned from the scars that rest upon your face?"

The bartender was startled by the stranger's question. She was unsure as to be upset by the direct nature of the question or to be humbled by the fact that someone actually took the time to really give her a second look and notice that she was aged beyond her years. She stayed silent at first. She spoke her possible responses to herself and quickly contemplated the tone of her reaction.

"Well mister, that's a deeply personal question. I don't feel comfortable answering a question such as that without even knowing the name of the person asking."

"If my question offends you, I apologize. You seem to be a very honest person who struggles with things such as belief and social education. I was just curious as to why that was and if perhaps the scars you wear bear any explanation. It is fair, however, to ask my name. I apologize for not properly introducing myself in the first place. I am Steve. A simple name for a simple man."

"A simple man eh? Well Steve, you seem to be a very upfront, no bullshit type of fella. I can respect that and let me tell ya, it aint too often I show respect for much", replied the bartender with an honest face.

There was a pause. Steve kept direct eye contact with the bartender awaiting the answer to his question. His face lacked emotion and intent. He wasn't just making small talk. The bartender felt compelled to unleash her truth upon her stranger. She never introduced herself formally as Steve had, but then again she never did for anyone. She always kept to herself, serving her drinks to her boys and taking in the banter from the bar.

"I can tell ya this Mr. Steve, I have earned these scars and believe me when I say that I have survived their stories. Some live through times, I have had the pleasure of surviving through times. Whether it was losing my baby or losing my love, I have been through the shit that these men around you still have coming to them. I stand behind this bar everyday and serve cheap liquor to the dead ash of the fire that burns over this town. I watch dreams die and people whither in poverty. I have seen the social devastation that will result in the end of our days and to be honest with ya mister, I aint the least bit scared. So what have my scars taught me ya ask? Well sir, they've taught me that hope is a waste of time and time is quickly running out. I feel sorry for those with hope. Look around ya mister, this is the death of humanity. I have learned that people kill people. They've tried to kill me, but I refuse to die. Only the sight of seeing the wretched burn at the end of the empty hour glass is keeping me alive."

Steve sat with his eyes still locked on the bartender. His face still stiff as stone as if not effected by the bartenders answer.

"If my answer offends you mister, I apologize. Now that you know me better than most, I have a question for you sir. What's your business here? I know all my boys and I have never seen ya before this day and I can't help but wonder what brings a fella as well put together as yourself into a dive like this?", asked the bartender with a determined aggression in her voice.

"My business you ask? Well miss, I am here looking for you", replied Steve.

"Me? Whatcha mean me?! I aint done nothing wrong mister, so if you're here looking for me you better start talking. This is no place for mystery. This is a place for the honest dead to rot away from the eyes of judgment. I take care of my boys and I know my boys. I don't, however, know you. With all due respect mister, I suggest you clue me in as to what you want from me."
The room took notice of the bartender's direct tone and now the stranger was on trial.

"I am here looking for you because I have a confession to make and I have chosen you to be my last judgment."

"Alright mister, I don't need any of that crazy shit up in here. If you don't tell me what this is all about, I'm gonna have to ask you to leave and trust me when I tell ya that there aint no where to go 'round here", demanded the bartender.

"I am the one responsible for what brings your boys to your bar. I am the one that set in motion the decline of economic stability. I am the one that brought upon the new death you were so excited for earlier and I am the one that put those scars upon your face", explained Steve in a slow, stutter free, heroic speech. "I am the second coming of the man who you once read about back when the sky had color and ignorance was bliss. I am the judgment. My purpose is my confession. I have been searching for the one that to carry my burden and for that reason, I sit before you here today. To live with little means just as our savior had done has proven to bring out the worst in man. To you and these boys of yours, poverty is a social status comparable to that of a sewer rat. To great men, it is a test of ones strength and courage. I have learned that the weak have indeed infested this place and great men have become nothing more than statistics for news media to profit on. This new death you spoke of is nothing more than a judgement. Look at those who have fallen. On the surface they are like everyone else. They enjoy a cup of coffee with the morning paper and tell stories of their day to their spouse at the dinner table. They also, however, lived lives of greed and lust. The judgment takes those who are weak. My business here is test the worth of man. Mankind has failed. They have failed to live through the steps of the man who gave his flesh for their redemption. What happens now is your business. You are the one who gives purpose to the fallen. You stand behind your bar and serve your drinks without prejudice but always a great sense of social awareness. You are now the messenger who will carry on the work and word of the creator. Your scars will heal and your heart will beat again. You will find the lost hope of man and you will restore the faith in the purpose. To answer your question directly miss, my business is now your business and you will find that lost love of yours again."

Steve then stood from his bar stool and reached into the front left pocket of his perfectly pleated slacks. His hand reappeared with a blade of sparkling silver. It was about the length of an unsharpened number 2 pencil. Steve raised it to his throat and with one swift motion, he slashed through his neck and dropped to the bar floor. No blood leaked from the wound but there was no life in the stranger as he lay motionless on the ground. No one in the room made a move to check for life. They all stood frozen in a state of shock and disbelief. The bartender's eyes were locked on the body. She had no emotion and a clean conscious. She raised a hand to her head and only young skin was there to touch. The scars had gone with the stranger.

Thank you for taking a dangerous ride with me...

Please exit to your right…

Watch your step!

Outspoken

So basically I'm just a punk with too much gunk floating around in my head! I've been told I'm a handful and too much to handle. I just like to have a good sober time. If it's just driving around in the car screaming my lungs out to a good Paramore song when the windows are rolled down with Jayme or jumping on my trampoline so be it. I'm the kind of girl who rather read a book than watch a movie, falls asleep early and wakes up early, eats desserts first, appetizer second and meal last, I don't change for anyone because I like my LOUD self the way I am, I'm not the cutest person in the world but I work with what I have, I'm defiantly the kind of person that will start a conversation with ANYONE, I'm awkward to the max but I think I work it well, I'm spastic but I honestly have a good heart, people can only describe me in one way "ahhhh" no other way or words will give it justice.